BAREFOOT SOULS

Maram al-Masri
Barefoot Souls
أرواح حافية

translated by Theo Dorgan

PUBLICATIONS
2015

Published by Arc Publications,
Nanholme Mill, Shaw Wood Road
Todmorden OL14 6DA, UK
www.arcpublications.co.uk

978 1910345 37 5 (pbk)
978 1910345 38 2 (hbk)
978 1910345 39 9 (ebook)

Design by Tony Ward
Cover design by Tony Ward & Ben Styles
Printed in Great Britain by
TJ International, Padstow, Cornwall

Supported using public funding by
ARTS COUNCIL
LOTTERY FUNDED ENGLAND

'Arc Translations'
Series Editor: Jean Boase-Beier

Pour ceux à qui l'histoire est aveugle
For those to whom history is blind

CONTENTS

Translator's Preface / 8
Author's Introduction –
'The Genesis of a Poem' / 10

رأيتهن / 12 • 'Je les ai vues.' • 'I have seen
them.' / 13

I
I Saw Them

بيتي / 16 • Betty / 17
كاترين / 20 • Catherine / 21
فرنسواز / 22 • Françoise / 23
فاطمة / 26 • Fatima / 27
غلاديس / 30 • Gladis / 31
عاطفة / 34 • Atifé / 35
جوسلين / 36 • Jocelyne / 37
اميناتا / 38 • Aminata / 39
سوسن / 40 • Sawsan / 41
مدام شارل / 42 • Madame Charles / 43
مدام شيفرو / 44 • Madame Chevrot / 45
نسيمة / 48 • Nassima / 49
شنتال / 50 • Chantal / 51
جورجيت / 52 • Georgette / 53
فيكتوريا / 54 • Victoria / 55
سونيا / 60 • Sonia / 61
أغنيسكا / 62 • Agnieska / 62
خديجة / 64 • Khadija / 65
مادلين / 68 • Madeleine / 69
خيرة / 70 • Khaïra / 71
تمارا / 72 • Tamara / 73
هيلينا / 74 • Helena / 75
نعيمة / 76 • Naïma / 77
مونيكا والأخريات / 78 • Monica et les autres • Monica and the
Others / 79

الحجاب / 80 • Voile • Veil / 81

غزة / 84 • Gaza / 85

II
THE SCREAM

فلورا / 90 • Flora / 91

سيف / 92 • Sef / 93

سارة / 94 • Sara / 95

بارتروك / 96 • Bartosh / 97

فادي / 98 • Faâdi / 99

سلمى / 100 • Salma / 101

سمير / 102 • Samir / 103

كليمان و رومان / 104 • Clément and Romain / 105

كلوة / 106 • Chloë / 107

III
WITH EVERY BEGINNING

الحب / 110 • L'amour • Love / 111

هن / 128 • Ce sont elles... • There are
Women / 129

أريد أن أكون / 130 • Je voudrais être une femme • I would like
to be a woman / 131

أشكرهم جميعهم / 132 • Merci à tous ceux... • I thank them
all / 133

Biographical Notes / 134

Homo sum, humani nihil a me alienum puto
PUBLIUS TERENTIUS AFER

The Roman playwright known to the Anglophone world as Terence was a freed slave whose six extant comedies are written in a plain, direct style. The quotation most frequently attributed to him, from the play *Heauton Timorumenos* (The Self Tormentor), translates simply as "I am human, nothing human is alien to me."

This phrase has been constantly at the back of my mind as I worked at translating these poems of Maram al-Masri's.

It is audacious enough of al-Masri to project herself into so many different selves, to present us with poems that speak for others, mainly women, in the poet's singular voice, but also in the individual voices of her personae, real or imagined. Each separate poem must convince the reader or listener that they are in the presence of a particular person, are witness to the testimony of a unique life. This has to be done despite the inescapable trace presence in every single poem of the poet's own, undeniable, sensibility.

Because al-Masri has chosen to write these poems in clear and direct French, it should be possible, I thought at first, to translate her almost word-for-word — and of course I have tried to find in English a register that answers to the apparent simplicity of the poems in French.

The difficulty, as is always the case with translations, has been almost entirely a question of finding the right, or the best possible, tone of voice. In other words, al-Masri's technical problem was to find a voice adequate to expressing such a diversity of other voices while allowing her own singular sensibility to come through, and mine has been to find a voice in English that answers to those ante-

8

cedent imperatives, a tone in Engish as fluent and credible as that found by al-Masri in French.

I was drawn to these poems by their stark simplicity, of a kind not often found in English, but also by their humane narratives of concern and compassion for all those, especially women, who have suffered violence. The individual stories are, for the most part, particular to a culture that is not my own — not the worst reason for undertaking a work of translation. I took what warrant and comfort I could from the proposition that "nothing human is alien to me", and embarked on the work.

In her note prefacing this collection, Maram al-Masri says that she attempts to speak for all victims of violence: "It is not only women who are victims of violence but entire peoples, children, old people, the dominated, the humiliated of every kind, in every country."

I hope that she will feel I have done her, and her beautiful poems, justice.

Theo Dorgan

It is always difficult to recognize the moment that gives birth to a poem, and even more difficult to grasp all the circumstances that surround and accompany the moment. Even if one knows the date of its first draft, a poem is always a long story that comes finally to inscribe itself on a white page. A poem one may read in a few seconds or in a few minutes is the result of a process that may have unfolded over many years.

When I received my first blow, a blow that would be followed, alas, by many others, physical and moral, as is the case with numerous women on whom is practised always this or that form of corporal or mental cruelty... what did I do? I wept bitterly in my powerlessness, and still, today, when I feel anger at having to undergo what is imposed on me, I can do nothing but suffer and endure it. This has allowed me to have a more acute understanding of the human condition and to communicate more closely with all those, men and women, who suffer violence. It is not only women who are victims of violence but entire peoples, children, old people, the dominated, the humiliated of every kind, in every country.

The day I felt a hot liquid flow between my thighs, felt the fear of a young girl, I decided that nobody in this world would have the right to threaten me, not even with their voice. From that humiliation, from that suffering which I endured for so long, a suffering to which I add the raising of my first child, from all of this was born the woman I have become. A woman who will not strike a blow, but who understands that there is a way out, a sublimation of all this suffered misery.

This overcoming, this overmastering of the human condition by crossing through the feminine condition... this is poetry.

From this intuition was born in me the feeling that I

can participate in the life of all, that I can share in the joys and sorrows of all. It was an extraordinary revelation, that beauty does not exclude what is ugly but subsumes and overcomes it.

I was astonished when the poem 'Women like me' was chosen in Palestine, in Ramallah, for inclusion in an educational programme for 12-18 year olds, astonished, too, when that poem was chosen in France for second-ary school classes where a student could speak of having been raped. I understood then that poetry can be a mirror to all, a mirror for all, that in poetry we may find healing.

Maram al-Masri
translated by Theo Dorgan

رأيتهن
هن
ووجوههن الزرقاء المموهة
هن
والكدمات المخفية بين
سيقانهن
هن
و كلماتهن الخرساء،
وأحلامهن المسجونة
هن
وابتساماتهن الواهنه و أيديهن
المرتجفة.

رأيت
تلك النساء
يعبرن الشارع كأرواح حافية
الأقدام
يلتفتن إلى الوراء
خائفات أن تلحقهن أقدام
العاصفة

سارقات القمر
يعبرن متنكرات
بنساء عاديات
لا يثرن الشبهات
سوى لمن
يشبههن

Je les ai vues.
Elles,
leurs visages aux bleus camouflés.
Elles,
leurs meurtrissures cachées entre les cuisses,
Elles,
leurs rêves capturés, leurs mots muets
Elles,
leurs sourires fatigués

Je les ai vues
toutes
passer dans la rue
âmes aux pieds nus,
regardant derrière elles,
inquiètes d'être suivies
par les pieds de la tempête,
voleuses de lune
elles traversent,
déguisées en femmes normales.
Personne ne peut les reconnaître
sauf celles
qui leur ressemblent.

I have seen them.
Those women
with faces camouflaged in blue,
those women
with bruises hidden between their thighs,
their dreams captured, their words silenced,
those women
with their weary smiles.

I have seen them
all
pass by in the street,
barefoot souls
looking over their shoulders,
worried about being followed,
fearing the footsteps of some storm;
thieves of the moon, they pass
in the guise of ordinary women.
Nobody can recognise them
except for those
who are of their kind.

I
I Saw Them

BETTY

Père	:	Georges
Mère	:	Emma
Âge	:	83 ans
Profession	:	ancienne institutrice

Betty
a une chatte.
Elle s'appelle
Katheline.
Katheline, la chatte de Betty
est détestée de tout le monde
sauf de
Betty
qui n'aime que
Katheline

Betty
ne fait rien
sauf s'asseoir devant sa fenêtre
à caresser la fourrure
de sa chatte maligne,
Katheline

Katheline
qui déteste tout le monde sauf
Betty.
Mais Betty s'attache
à tenir chaque jour
son journal intime,
l'unique chose qui la distrait
de Katheline.

بيتي

اسم الاب: جورج
الأُم: ايما
العمر: 83 عاماً
المهنة: مدرسة في الأبتدائي
سابقا

بيتي،
عندها قطة اسمها
كاتلين.
الجميع يكره كاتلين قطة
بيتي
سوى بيتي التي لا تحب سوى
كاتلين

بيتي
لا تفعل شيئا في نهارها
عدا الجلوس أمام النافذة
تمسد وبر القطة اللعوب
كاتلين
كاتلين
التي تكره الجميع عدا
بيتي
إلا أن بيتي
حريصة كل الحرص
أن تكتب يومياتها
وهذا هو الأمر الوحيد الذي
يلهيها عن
كاتلين

16

BETTY

Father	:	Georges
Mother	:	Emma
Age	:	83
Occupation	:	Retired schoolmistress

Betty
has a cat,
she calls her
Katheline.
Betty's cat
is detested by everyone
except by Betty
who loves nobody
except Katheline.

Betty
does nothing all day
except sit by the window
caressing the fur
of her malign cat,
Katheline,

Katheline
who detests everyone except
Betty.
Betty diligently
keeps up her daily diary,
the only thing that distracts her
from Katheline.

Samedi: Katheline ne mange pas.
Dimanche: Katheline a mangé deux
      souris.
Lundi: Katheline miaule beaucoup.
Mardi: Katheline me regarde avec
      amour.
Mercredi: Katheline a perdu quelques
      poils.
Jeudi: Katheline...
Vendredi: Katheline...   Katheline...
      K a t h e .

السبت: كاتلين لم تأكل
جيداً
الأحد: أكلت كاتلين
صحنين
الإثنين: كاتلين تنوء كثيراً
الثلاثاء: كاتلين نظرت إلي
بحب هذا الصباح
الأربعاء: كاتلين فقدت قليلا
مَن وبرها
الخميس: كاتلين . . .
الجمعة . . . . كاتلين
كاتلين
كا ت ل ي ن
كات

Saturday:	Katheline's not eating
Sunday:	Katheline ate two mice
Monday:	Katheline miaowing a lot
Tuesday:	Katheline looking at me lovingly
Wednesday:	Katheline has lost a few hairs
Thursday:	Katheline...
Friday:	Katheline... Katheline...

K a t h e .

CATHERINE

Mère	: Jeannette
Père	: Jean-Claude
Âge	: 48 ans
Profession	: femme au foyer

كاترين

الأم: جانيت
الأب: جان كلود
العمر: 48
المهنة: زوجة في البيت

Peut-être,
parce qu'elle est si féminine
si pleine de désirs,
Catherine la Blonde
donne-t-elle à penser
qu'elle est frivole.
Mais ce n'est qu'une femme
remplie de tendresse
qui aime ses enfants
et range sa maison tous les matins.

لعل كاترين الشقراء
طافحة الأنوثة والشهوة
التي تثير الظن بأنها لعوب
ليست سوى امرأة
فائقة اللطف
تحب أطفالها
وترتب بيتها كل صباح

Privée d'amour
elle en cherche dans les yeux des
    passants
ou du conducteur de bus.
Elle mendie
du trottoir un sourire.
Et à chaque carrefour
elle attend
un miracle.

محرومة من الحب
مهجورة
تفتش عنه في عيون المارة
وسائقي الباصات
تتسول ابتسامة من الأرصفة
وتنتظر
عند كل مفرق
معجزة

CATHERINE

Mother   : Jeanette
Father   : Jean-Claude
Age   : 48
Occupation : Housewife

Perhaps
because she is so feminine,
so full of desires,
Catherine the Blonde
gives the impression
that she is frivolous.
But she is only a woman
filled with tenderness,
who loves her children
and tidies her house every morning.

Deprived of love
she searches for it in the eyes of passers by,
in the eyes of the bus driver.
She begs
a smile from the pavement,
at every crossroad
expects
a miracle.

FRANÇOISE

Mère	:	Marie
Père	:	Alain
Âge	:	42 ans
Profession	:	bibliothécaire

فرنسواز

اسم الأم: ماري
اسم الأب: آلان
العمر: 42 سنة
المهنة: موظفة في مكتبة

Cette chaise
est pour moi.
Je l'ai portée à pied de la boutique
jusqu'à la maison.

هذا الكرسي لي
حملته من عند البائع
إلى البيت.

Ce chandelier en argent
est un cadeau
d'une amie.

هذا الشمعدان الفضي
هدية من صديقتي

Ce miroir,
je l'ai hérité de ma famille.
Il était au centre du mur de l'entrée.
Et comme j'ai dansé devant
quand j'étais petite!

هذه المرآة
أتيت بها من بيت أهلي
كانت تتصدر حائط المدخل
وكم كنت أرقص أمامها وأنا
صغيرة

Tu peux garder le canapé.
De toute façon, c'est toi
qui t'allongeais dessus
pendant des jours et des nuits
devant des films
que tu regardais
tout seul.

لك الاحتفاظ بالأريكة
فعلى كل حال
أنت من تمدد عليها
طيلة أيام وليال
أمام الأفلام التي كنت تراها
لوحدك

Tu peux prendre la télé, le frigidaire,
les casseroles, les couteaux, les
     fourchettes,
le lit et aussi les rideaux si tu veux
(Pourtant c'est moi qui les ai cousus).

لك أن تأخذ التلفزيون والبراد
الطناجر والملاعق
السرير والستائر إن رغبت
مع العلم بأنني أنا من حاكها

22

FRANÇOISE

Mother   : Marie
Father   : Alain
Age   : 42
Occupation : Librarian

This chair
is for me.
I carried it on foot from the shop
to the house.

That silver candlestick
was a gift
from a woman friend.

This mirror
I inherited from my family,
it hung in the centre of the wall
in the entrance hall.

Oh how I danced before it
when I was small!

You can keep the couch,
after all it's you
who'd stretch out on it
all those days and nights
in front of those films
you would watch
all on your own.

You can have the TV, the fridge,
the pots and pans, the knives, the forks,
the bed, and the curtains if you wish
(even though it was I who sewed them).

أما البيت
فلنتقاسمه
انت دفعت ثمنه مالا
وأنا دفعت ثمنه حرمانا
ولي به أيام تعب ووجع ظهر

فقط
دع لي الأطفال. .

Quant à la maison,
on la partage.
Toi tu l'as payée en argent
et moi
je l'ai payée de mes privations.
En elle
j'ai laissé bien des jours de fatigue
et de mal au dos.

Mais
laisse-moi les enfants.

As for the house,
we'll split it.
You paid for it in money
and I,
I paid with my sufferings
in it.
There I spent many an exhausting day,
crippled with pains in my back.

Just,
leave me the children.

FATIMA

Mère	:	Souâd
Père	:	Osmane
Âge	:	23 ans
Profession	:	étudiante en littérature

À douze ans,
elle devint femme.

Sa mère la coinça dans un coin
pour lui faire comprendre que désormais
elle était
apte au mariage et à l'enfantement.
Et que, dès lors,
et pour toute sa vie,
elle devait renoncer à jouer
avec les garçons du quartier.

À douze ans
son histoire de femme commença.

Sa grand-mère
lui parla d'une fleur entre ses cuisses,
fine comme du papier à cigarette
qui ne flambe qu'une fois.

Depuis l'âge de douze ans
chaque mois,
Elle pleure à cause d'un mal mystérieux
dans son ventre
et d'un douloureux désire de jouer,
malgré la peur
de voir sa fleur se déchirer.

فاطمة

اسم الام: سعاد
الأب: عثمان
العمر: 23
المهنة: طالبة آداب

في الثانية عشرة من عمرها
أصبحت امرأة.
حشرتها أمها في الزاوية
لتفهمها
بأنها أصبحت صالحة للزواج
والأنجاب
وبأنها من الآن وصاعدا
عليها الامتناع عن اللعب
مع صبيان الحارة.

في الثانية عشرة من عمرها
بدأ تاريخها كامرأة .
حدثتها جدتها عن غشاء بين
ساقيها
رقيق كورق السجائر

منذ الثانية عشرة بدأت تبكي
في كل شهر
لوجع غامض في بطنها
ولرغبتها في اللعب
رغم خوفها أن تتمزق ورقتها

FATIMA

Mother   : Souâd
Father   : Osmane
Age   : 23
Occupation : Student of Literature

At the age of twelve
she became a woman.

Her mother confined her to a corner
to make her understand that from now on
she is
eligible for marriage and childbearing.
From now on,
and for the rest of her life,
she has to give up playing
with the neighbourhood boys.

At the age of twelve,
her life as a woman began.

Her Grandmother
spoke to her of a flower between her thighs
as fine as a cigarette paper
that will flame only once.

From the age of twelve,
every month she weeps because of some mysterious pain
in her stomach,
and some sorrowful desire to play
despite the fear
of seeing her flower torn.

في كل شهر بدأت تنضج
في كل شهر بدأت تحرم
ووجع بطنها يزداد

لم تدرِ كم كان لها من
العمر
حين أهدت ورقتها لشاب
أحبته
ذهب بها بعيدا وتركها
بلا ثمن

بمال إسوارتها الذهبية
اشترت ورقة جديدة،
إلا أن طفولتها
فاطمة
لم تستطع أن تشتريها

Ainsi, mois après mois,
elle commença à mûrir,
puis, se mit à vieillir
et son mal de ventre
empira.

Elle ne sait plus qu'elle âge elle avait
quand elle décida d'offrir sa fleur
à un garçon qu'elle avait aimé.

Il est parti, loin,
la laissant,
sans valeur.

Avec l'argent de son bracelet en or
Fatima
put s'acheter
une autre virginité.

Mais son enfance
jamais
elle n'a pu la racheter.

Like this, month after month,
she began to ripen,
then she began to age
and her stomach pain
worsened.

She no longer knows what age she was
when she decided to offer her flower
to a boy she liked.

He is long gone,
leaving her
worthless.

With money from selling her gold bracelet
Fatima
can purchase
another virginity.

But her childhood,
that
she can never buy back.

GLADIS

Mère	:	Antigone
Père	:	Yannis
Âge	:	71 ans
Profession	:	sdf

Dans ses pieds, des milliers de pas et
    de directions.
Avec ses souliers de tissu léger
ornés d'une rose qui paraissent neufs
elle sillonne Paris enneigé.

Sur elle, un pré fleuri
de plusieurs vêtements d'été
enfilés les uns sur les autres
comme sur des cintres.

Sur ses épaules
elle a jeté avec majesté
un drap de laine noué autour du cou
comme Superman.
Dans chaque main, elle porte un sac de
    nylon
où elle a soigneusement rangé ses affaires.

Elle marche, le dos droit,
les yeux dans le vague,
comme si elle ne voyait personne.

Sous un escalier, à l'arrière d'un grand
    magasin
Gladis a installé sa salle à manger
où elle prépare ses plats biologiques
qu'elle mange lentement.

غلاديس

اسم الأم: انتيغون
اسم الأب: يانيس
العمر: 71
المهنة: بدون بيت

في قدمي غلاديس ملايين
الخطوات والاتجاهات
وحذاء من القماش الرقيق
مزين بوردة
يبدو جديدا
تعبر به باريس المثلجة

عليها ملابس صيفية مزهرة
لبستها فوق بعضها
جعلت منها حقلا.

على كتفيها رمت بجلالة
غطاءً صوفياً
تعقده كسوبرمان على رقبتها
بكلتا يديها تحمل كيسين من
النايلون
رتبت فيهما بعناية حوائجها.

بعيون زائغة وظهر مستقيم
تمشي غلاديس وكأنها لا ترى
أحدا.

جعلت من السلم الخلفي
للمخزن الكبير
غرفةً لطعامها
تفرد فيها زوادتها
وتأكل أطباقها البيولوجية
على مهل

GLADIS

Mother   :   Antigone
Father   :   Yannis
Age   :   71
Occupation :   Homeless person

In her feet, thousands of steps and directions.
In her light cloth shoes,
new-seeming, rose-ornamented,
she travels snowbound Paris.

She wears a flowering meadow
of many summer dresses,
layered one above the other
as if on hangers.

Over her shoulders
she has majestically draped
a wool curtain, fastened at the neck
like Superman's cloak.
In each hand she carries a nylon sack
in which she has carefully arranged her possessions.

Back straight,
she walks with her eyes unfocused,
as if seeing no-one.

Under some steps, behind a Department Store,
Gladis has set up her dining room
where she prepares the organic meals
she will eat slowly.

ومن كابين التليفون
غرفةً لنومها .

غلاديس تتحدث كسيدة
صالون
لا تحب تذكر ماضيها
تكتفي بالقول بإنها
مرت بظروف صعبة جعلتها
بدون مأوى بدون سرير
بدون أهل
بدون أصداقاء
ولكن لديها مشروع
مشروع رقص على المسرح
سيتحقق يوما
س ي ت ح ق ق

Et elle a transformé une cabine télé-
phonique
en chambre à coucher.

Gladis parle avec l'élégance d'une
femme de salons.
elle n'aime pas qu'on évoque son passé.
Elle est content de dire qu'elle a connu
des moments difficiles,
et c'est pourquoi elle est
sans lit,
sans famille,
sans amis,
mais elle a un projet: danser sur scène.
Un projet qu'un jour,
elle va réaliser,
réa
-liser.

She has transformed a telephone kiosk
into her bedroom.

Gladis chats with the elegance of a fashionable woman.
She does not care to have her past brought up.
She will concede that she has known
some difficult moments,
and this is why she is
without a bed,
without a family,
without friends,
but she has a plan: to dance on stage.
A plan she will one day realise,
                              rea
                                    -lise.

ATIFÉ

Mère	:	décédée
Père	:	Safar Ali
Âge	:	16 ans
Pays	:	Iran
Profession	:	la mort ne l'a pas laissée travailler

عاطفة

الأم: يتيمة
الأب: سفر علي
العمر: 16
إيران
المهنة لم يسمح لها الموت
أن تعمل

Est-ce que c'est un crime
si mes pieds sont joyeux de toucher l'essence
de la Terre
quand je danse?

هل هي جريمة
أن تفرح قدمي برائحة الارض
وأنا أرقص؟

Est-ce que c'est un crime
si je découvre mes épaules
et laisse flotter mes cheveux?

هل هي جريمة
أن أمنح للهواء كتفي
وأبعثر شعري على ظهري؟

Est-ce que c'est un crime
de mettre du rouge à lèvres
et de dire que j'ai une bouche?

هل هي جريمة
أن أضع حمرة الشفاه
وأقول أنا صبية ككل صبايا
العالم
لدي فم
لدي جسد؟. .

Est-ce un crime
si je suis une fille
comme toutes les autres filles du monde?

هل هي جريمة
ان ارقص
أن أكتب
أن أغني
أن أرغب
أن أحب

Si j'ai un corps,
si je dors
si je chante
si j'écris
si j'ai des désirs
si j'aime?

هل هي جريمة أن أولد
في بلد يشنق عنق الحرية؟

Est-ce un crime de vivre dans un pays
où on pend par le cou
la liberté?

34

ATIFÉ

Mother   :   deceased
Father   :   Safar Ali
Age   :   16
Country   :   Iran
Occupation :   Death has not permitted her to work

Is it a crime
if my feet are happy to touch the essence
of Earth
when I dance?

Is it a crime,
to bare my shoulders,
to let my hair float free?

Is it a crime
to put colour on my lips,
to say I have a mouth?

Is it a crime
that I am no more than a girl
like all the other girls in the world,

That I have a body,
that I sleep,
that I sing,
that I write,
that I have desires,
that I love?

Is it a crime to live in a country
where freedom
is hanged by the neck?

Mère   : Jacqueline
Père   : Roland
Âge   : 35 ans
Profession : assistante maternelle

جوسلين

الأم: جاكلين
الأب: رولان
العمر: 35
المهنة: مدرسة

Je rentre dans notre chambre
comme si j'entrais dans un lieu de culte.
Je me lave avec de l'eau
qui ressemble à des larmes.

Je suis là.
Tu n'as pas besoin de frapper avant
    d'entrer.

أدخل غرفتنا
وكأني أدخل معبدا
اغتسل بماء
يشبه الدموع .

أنا هنا
ليس هناك حاجة أن تطرق
لكي تدخل

Toute chose t'attend
même les moustiques que j'ai essayé
    de chasser
avec de l'encens.

Toute chose t'attend
jusqu'au duvet de mon ventre.

كل شيء ينتظرك
حتى البعوضة التي حاولت
طردها
بالبخور .

كل شيء ينتظر
حتى وبر البطن
ثم
أهيّئ سريرنا
وأنام
وحيدة. . .

Puis,
je prépare notre lit
et je dors
seule.

JOCELYNE

Mother	:	Jacqueline
Father	:	Roland
Age	:	35
Occupation	:	Childminder

I return to our room
as if entering a cult chamber.
I wash myself with water
that resembles tears.

I am here,
you do not need to knock before you enter.

Everything awaits you,
even the mosquitoes I've tried to banish
by burning incense.

Everything awaits you,
even the soft down on my belly...

Then,
I prepare our bed
and I sleep
alone.

AMINATA

Mère	:	Diatou
Père	:	Samba
Née	:	au Sénégal
Âge	:	45 ans
Profession	:	cuisinière

Elle disait
en désignant ce qu'il y a entre ses jambes:

«Ici
une douleur vivante
qui saigne
qui crie
qui pleure
Elle raconte l'histoire de la souffrance et
    de l'injustice.

Ils l'ont coupé
morceau par morceau.
Ils ont cousu sa bouche
afin que, nuit après nuit,
elle ne gémisse pas.

Ils ont chanté
       Ils ont dansé
              poussé des youyous
Ils ont dit fièrement:
"Nous avons coupé la tête de Satan."

Ils ont fait mourir la femme en moi.
Ils m'ont transformée
en cadavre
qui marche.»

اميناتا

الأم: دياتو
الاب: سامبا
العمر: 45
المهنة: طباخة

قالت وهي تشير إلى ما بين
ساقيها
هنا
يوجد ألم حيّ
ينز،
يصرخ،
يبكي
ويروي
تاريخ الألم والقهر

جزءا جزءا
قطعوه
خاطوا فمه
لئلا يئنّ كل مساء

غنوا
رقصوا ،
زغردوا

قالوا بفخر
بترنا رأس الشيطان

أماتوا المرأة التي بي
حولوني
لجثة تمشي

AMINATA

Mother   : Diatou
Father   : Samba
Born   : Senegal
Age   : 45
Occupation : Cook

She said,
referring to what's between her legs:

"Here
is a living sorrow
that bleeds,
that cries out,
that weeps,
that tells a story of suffering
                    and injustice.

They cut it away,
morsel by morsel.
They sewed up her mouth
so that, night after night,
she would not groan.

They sang,
        they danced,
                ululating,
they said, proudly:
'We have cut off the head of Satan.'

They have killed the woman in me,
they have transformed me
into a walking corpse."

SAWSAN

Mère	:	Djamila
Père	:	Khaled
Âge	:	34 ans
Profession	:	infirmière

Il attend que je me glisse
dans mon bain pour bloquer
tous les accès
même l'air.

Pluie de pierres
    de mots
        tempête de gifles.

Mon seul réflexe
est de mettre une main
sur la poitrine
et l'autre sur le bas du ventre
qu'un jour il cueillit en amant.

La salle de bain
était mon guérisseur
Son eau était
ma consolation.
Je m'absentais du monde
laissant les senteurs
soulager mes douleurs.
Et soudain
elle est
le
        p
          i
            è
              g
                e.

سوسن

الأم: جميلة
الأب: خالد
العمر: 34
المهنة: ممرضة

يستفرد بي
سادا
عليّ كل المنافذ
حتى الهواء .

مطر من صخر الكلام
عواصف من الصفعات

أضع يدا على صدري
وأخرى أغطي بها أسفل بطني
الذي استقبله يوما
كحبيب معشوق

الحمّام طبيبي
في مائه
أغرق همومي

أغيب به
تاركة الطيب
يداوي آلامي
فإذا
به
ال
كـ
مـ
ين.

SAWSAN

Mother	:	Djamila
Father	:	Khaled
Age	:	34
Occupation	:	Nurse

He waits until I slide
into my bath
to block all access,
even to air.

Rain of stones,
          of words,
                    a storm of slaps.

My only solace
is to place one hand
on my breast,
and the other below my belly
where once it was received
like a lover.

The bathroom
was once my healer,
its water
my consolation.
There I would absent myself from the world,
letting its scents
relieve my sorrows –
and suddenly,
that is
the
    t
      r
        a
           p.

MADAME CHARLES

Elle habite au bout du passage
Marie-Louise dans le 93.

De la fenêtre de sa maison blanche
elle surveille les passants
et les voleurs d'amour que ramène
   Marie-Pierre.
Chaque dimanche elle va à l'église
et chaque mardi le coiffeur refait sa
   coiffure.
Son mari l'a quittée
quand elle a eu cinquante ans.
Elle n'a pas connu d'autres hommes,
«À quoi servent-ils?»

Dans son agenda
beaucoup de dates d'anniversaires,
de fêtes et de projets pour les années
   à venir.
Elle fabrique des cakes et des bonbons
et parfois les vend.
Madame Charles aime les cadeaux,
surtout ceux qu'elle reçoit.
Madame Charles
a soigneusement rangé quatre-vingt-
   quinze ans
dans son armoire
et elle fait toujours des projets.

مدام شارل

تسكن في نهاية ممر ماري
لويز
في الدائرة الـ 93

من نافذة بيتها الأبيض
تراقب المارة
ولصوص الحب اللذين تأتي
بهم ماري بيير
كل أحد
تذهب الى الكنيسة
وكل ثلاثاء
يعيد الحلاق تسريحتها الأنيقة
هجرها زوجها
وعمرها خمسين عاما
لم تعرف رجالا غيره (فما
نفعهم)

في رزنامتها
مواعيد كثيرة ومشاريع
لسنوات قادمة
تصنع الحلوى وأحيانا تبيعها
تحب الهدايا وخاصة التي
تتلقاها

مدام شارل
في خزانتها رتبت بعناية
خمسة وتسعين سنة
وما تزال تخطط

42

MADAME CHARLES

She lives at the back of the passage Marie-Louise
in the 93rd (Seine-Saint-Denis)

From the window of her white house
she surveys the passers-by
and the thieves of love who brought down Marie-Pierre.
Every Sunday she goes to church
and every Tuesday the hairdresser resets her perm.
Her husband left her
when she was fifty.
She has not known other men –
'What would be the point?'

In her diary,
the dates of many birthdays,
holidays and projects for the coming year.
She makes cakes and sweets,
sometimes she sells them.
Madame Charles loves presents,
she especially loves receiving them.
Madame Charles
has carefully arranged her 95 years
in her cabinet,
and is always making plans.

Âge   : 75 ans
Profession : ancienne teinturière

مدام شيفرو

العمر: 75
المهنة: غسالة ألبسة

منذ مدة
لم أر مدام شيفرو
المرأة التي كنت أصادف
في الشارع الرئيسي

ابتسامتها لي
تجبرني على التوقف
رغم عجلتي
للحديث عن الطقس
عن جمالها الغابر
وعن الرجال الذين أحبوها.

مدام شيفرو قصيرة القامة
ذات أنف عريض باذنجاني
وأسنان قليلة
مكسورة وسوداء
تحلف بفخر أنها طبيعية.

أنيقة ما أتاح لها عمرها
متبرجة حتى أن جفنيها
يتدليان من ثقل
الكحل

في لقاءنا الأخير
أخبرتني بأنها
تعرفت على رجل في صالة
الرقص
حيث تتعلم الصلصة

Il y a longtemps
que je n'ai pas vu madame Chevrot,
la femme que j'avais l'habitude
de rencontrer dans la rue principale.

Elle me souriait
et son sourire m'obligeait à m'arrêter,
même si j'étais pressée,
pour parler du temps,
de sa beauté jadis
et des hommes qui l'ont aimée.

Madame Chevrot est petite,
un nez gros comme une aubergine
et quelques dents
cassées et noires.
Elle jure, avec fierté, qu'elles sont vraies.

Élégante, autant que l'âge le lui permet.
Maquillée, jusqu'à en faire tomber ses
        paupières…
Lors de notre dernière rencontre
elle m'a raconté
qu'elle a fait la connaissance d'un homme
dans la salle de danse
où elle apprend la salsa.

Il voudrait tant vivre avec elle…
Mais elle?
Elle hésite,

MADAME CHEVROT

Age   : 75
Occupation : Former dyer & colourist

It's been a long time
since I laid eyes on Madame Chevrot,
a woman I used to see
on the main street.

She would smile at me
and her smile would oblige me to stop,
even if I was in a hurry,
to talk about the weather,
her faded beauty,
the men who'd once loved her.

Madame Chevrot is petite,
a big nose like an aubergine
and a few teeth,
broken and black –
she swears, proudly, that they're her own.

Elegant, inasmuch as her age permits.
Made-up, even to her fluttering eyelids.

At our last encounter
she told me
she'd made the acquaintance of a man
at the dance hall
where she's learning salsa.

He really wants to live with her…
But Madame,
she's hesitating,

partagée entre renoncer à sa liberté
ou renoncer à ses ronflements,
car, dit-elle,
c'est tout ce qu'il lui apporte,
la nuit.

ويرغب أن يعيش معها.

حائرة بين أن تهجر حريتها
أو أن تهجر شخيره
فكما تقول
هذا كل ما يمنحها إياه
ليلا.

between giving up her freedom
or accepting him and his snoring –
because that
is all he brings with him
at night.

NASSIMA

Mère	:	Rachida
Père	:	Mohamed
Née	:	à Rabat
Âge	:	25 ans
Vit à Paris 19^e		
Profession	:	sans emploi

Sur la tête de Nassima, une blessure,
   trois points de suture

Nassima,
dans sa tête poussaient des rêves
            des poèmes d'amour
                        et des souhaits
quand pour la première fois
elle a revêtue sa robe blanche.

Cela fait maintenant un an
que Nassima est enfermée dans sa maison,
comme une poupée
dans un coffre à jouets.

Sa maison est sa tombe.
C'est elle qui en a cousu les rideaux
avec les mains de sa patience.
C'est elle qui en a essuyé le sol à genoux.
Elle qui s'est protégée derrière ses murs,
derrière ses portes…

Sa maison,
avec ses fenêtres toujours fermées,
est son témoin
silencieux.

نسيمة

اسم الأم: رشيدة
اسم الأب: محمد
العمر: 25
مواليد: الرباط
الإقامة: باريس المنطقة 19
المهنة: عاطلة عن العمل

في رأسها، نسيمة،
جرح
ثلاث قطبات وأوهام مهشمة

في رأسها نسيمة
أحلام
أشعار حب
وأمنيات
عندما لبست فستانها الأبيض
ورقصت .

سنة كاملة
ونسيمة مخبّئة
كلعبة في علبة.
بيتها قبرها
خيطت ستائره بأصابع
صبرها
مسحت أرضه على ركبتيها
احتمت بحيطانه
ووراء أبوابه .

بيتها ذو النوافذ المغلقة أبدا
شاهد أخرس
على موتها.

NASSIMA

Mother   : Rachida
Father   : Mohamed
Born   : Rabat
Age   : 25
Lives in Paris 19ᵉ
Occupation : Unemployed

On Nassima's head, a scar,
        three stitches.

Nassima is cultivating dreams in her head,
                love poems
                        and wishes
since for the first time
she put on her white robe.

It is already a year
that Nassima is locked up in her house
like a doll
in a box of toys.

Her house is her tomb,
she herself has sewn the curtains
with her patient hands,
it is she who has washed the floor, on her knees,
she who is protected behind the walls,
behind the doors.

Her house,
with its permanently closed windows,
is her silent witness.

CHANTAL

شنتال

Mère　　　：Patricia
Père　　　：Jean
Âge　　　：42 ans
Sans profession
Signe particulier : aucun

الأم: باتريسيا
الأب: جان
العمر: 42
المهنة: بدون
العلامة الفارقة: لايوجد

Ceci, c'est une porte
de ce côté, la porte de la maison,
de ce côté, la porte du monde.
Ceci, c'est l'escalier
de ce côté, l'escalier qui conduit au
　　　silence,
de ce côté, l'escalier qui conduit au
　　　soleil.
Ceci est un salon
Il contient un canapé où personne ne
　　　s'allonge,
des fenêtres qui restent toujours
　　　fermées,
une table autour de laquelle personne
　　　ne s'assoit.
Ici, c'est la chambre des enfants
elle contient leurs socquettes et leurs
　　　chemises,
leurs rêves et leur odeur aussi.

Ici, c'est la chambre des parents
où n'entre plus
ni soleil ni lune.

هذا باب
باب البيت من هذه الجهة
وباب العالم من تلك الجهة
هذا سلم
سلم يؤدي إلى الصمت من
هذه الجهة
وسلم يؤدي إلى الشمس من
تلك الجهة
هذه غرفة الاستقبال
بها أريكة ونوافذ تبقى أحيانا
مغلقة
وطاولة لا يجتمع حولها أحد
هنا غرفة الأطفال
بها قمصاهم وجواربهم
بها أحلامهم
ورائحتهم

هنا غرفة الوالدين حيث
لا شمس
و لا قمر

CHANTAL

Mother   : Patricia
Father   : Jean
Age   : 42
No occupation
Special sign : None

This, this is a door.
On this side the front door,
on this side the door of the world.
This, this is the stairs.
On this side the stairs leading to silence,
on this side the stairs leading to the sun.
This is a living room,
it contains a couch where nobody ever stretches out,
windows that are always shut,
a table around which nobody ever sits.
Here is the children's room,
it holds their ankle socks, their shirts,
their dreams and their smells.

Here, here is the parents' room
where the sun and the moon
no longer enter.

GEORGETTE

Mère   :   Marie
Père   :   Elias
Âge   :   50 ans
Profession :   patronne de restaurant

جورجيت

الأم: ماري
الأب: الياس
العمر: 50
العمل: صاحبة مطعم

لم تكن تدري عندما قالت
نعم
أنها ستقول
لا
بعد عشرين سنة
وحيدة ستصارع وحوش
الحياة
هي التي على مفرق العمر
تقف بتجاعيدها
بحيضها الأخير
أمام الأمل
عاشق الشباب

تعبة
تتأرجح على الحافة
لكنها تغمض عينيها
وتقفز

Elle ne savait pas quand elle a dit
   «oui»
que, vingt ans après, elle dirait «non».
Seule, elle va combattre les fauves de
   la vie.

Elle, la fatiguée
Elle, qui s'arrête aux carrefours de l'âge
Elle, qui affronte
avec ses rides
ses dernières règles,
l'espoir,
ce jeune amant.

Fatiguée,
elle vacille
sur le rebord
elle ferme les yeux et
s'élance.

GEORGETTE

Mother	:	Marie
Father	:	Elias
Age	:	50
Occupation	:	Restaurant owner

She did not know when she said 'yes'
that twenty years later she would say 'no'.
Alone, she must struggle with the beasts.

She, the exhausted one,
she, halted at the crossroads of life,
she, who confronts with her wrinkles
her final menses,
hope,
this young lover.

Exhausted,
teetering on the edge,
she closes her eyes
and she soars.

VICTORIA

Mère   : Piera
Père   : Antonello
Âge   : 43 ans
Profession : fonctionnaire

فيكتوريا

الأسم: فيكتوريا
الام: بيرا
الاب: انطونيلو
العمر: 43
المهنة: موظفة

I

Cela fait dix ans que nous dormons
     dans le même lit
avec des pieds qui ne se touchent plus.
Dix ans que mes yeux ne l'ont pas vu
et que mes oreilles n'ont pas été
     caressées par son souffle.

II

Il paraît que des fois
je laisse traîner mes vêtements intimes,
C'est vrai
c'est arrivé quatre fois, peut-être cinq,
durant tout ma vie avec lui.
Un jour , il cria:
«Ta mère ne t'a pas appris
que tu dois cacher ces choses-là?»
Et comment voulez-vous que j'imagine
qu'il irait rechercher dans la poubelle
mes serviettes hygiéniques?
Car c'est arrivé, ça aussi;
j'ai jeté mes serviettes dans la poubelle.

1

منذ أكثر من عشرة سنوات
ونحن ننام في سرير
واحد
بقدمين لا يتلامسان
عشرة سنوات لم تقع عينه
علي
ولا استقبلت أذناي أنفاسه

2

يبدو أنني أنسى أحيانا
ملابسي الداخلية على
مرأى البصر
صحيح!
حصل أن نسيتها ثلاث
مرات ربما؟؟
لنقل خمس مرات طيلة حياتنا
معا.
فينهرني غاضبا. .
ألم تعلمك أمك بأنه عليك
أن تخفي هذه الأشياء؟
كيف لي أن أتوقع أنه
سيفتش في سلة
الزبالة ؟
حصل هذا ايضا،
رميت الفوطة في سلة الزبالة

54

VICTORIA

Mother   : Piera
Father   : Antonello
Age   : 43
Occupation : Public servant

I

It has been ten years since we slept in the one bed,
our feet never touching.
Ten years since I laid eyes on him,
since my ears were caressed by his breathing.

II

It seems that sometimes I let fall
my intimate apparel.
It's true,
this happened four times, perhaps five,
during my whole life with him.
One day, he cried out:
'Didn't your mother ever tell you
to conceal those things?'
And how could I have imagined
he would go through the rubbish bin,
finding my sanitary towels?
Because that also happened;
I threw my sanitary towels in the bin.

III

D'habitude c'est lui qui suspend le linge.
Moi, je trouve que c'est une perte de temps.
Une fois, il a pris un slip où la trace était
    incrustée, parce qu'il étai vieux
ou que l'eau était trop chaude.
«Tu n'as pas honte?»
Et il me rappelle pourquoi il ne m'a pas
    touchée depuis dix ans
en secouant cette petite chose dans ses
    mains
et en me la jetant au visage.

IV

Un jour,
j'ai pris mon courage dans ma bouche
et j'ai répondu: «Non, je n'ai pas honte.
Quelle honte je devrais avoir
d'être une femme?
Oui, je suis une femme
comme toutes les femmes.
Je saigne une fois par mois
et ça s'appelle les règles.»
Et il peut bien me virer de son lit
s'il a peur que je le tache...

3

عادة هو من ينشر الغسيل
غالبا ما أجد ذلك مضيعة
للوقت،
وخاصة عندما يكون لدي
مائة عمل أهم من
وضع الغسيل على
الحبال.
فيخرج كلسونا ما تزال عليه
بقع حتى بعد غسله
لأنه قديم أو لأن الماء لم
يكن ساخناً
فيناديني قائلاً
ألا تخجلين؟
مذكرا إياي بأنني لم أدرك
حتى الآن لماذا لم يعد
يلمسني.
ملوحا لي بهذا الشيء
وقاذفا إياه في وجهي.

4

ذات يوم
استجمعت شجاعتي في
فمي رادة
عليه
لست أخجل
فأي عار أرتكبه بكوني امرأة؟
أنا امرأة كك النساء
أنزف دما مرة في الشهر
وهذا اسمه العادة الشهرية
وباستطاعته طردي من سريره
اذا رغب
خوفا ان ألوثه
و

56

III

Normally, it is he who hangs out the washing.
Me, I think it's a waste of time.
One time he found a slip where the stain
had dried in, because it was old
or because the water had been too hot.
'Have you no shame?'
And he reminded me why he hadn't touched me
these past ten years,
shaking that little slip in his hands,
throwing it in my face.

IV

One day,
I summoned the courage to answer,
to say 'No, I'm not ashamed.
What shame should I feel
for being a woman?
Yes, I am a woman
like all other women.
I bleed once every month
and these are called periods',
and he could throw me out of his bed
if he feared I might stain it...

Bien sûr, à partir de ce moment-là,
il ne m'a pas laissée laver mon linge
dans la même machine que lui.
J'attends qu'il ne soit pas à la maison
pour l'utiliser.
Pas parce que je veux
qu'il me touche à nouveau.
Mais parce qu'il est devenu un étranger
après avoir été
mon mari.

طبعا من حينها
لم أغسل حوائجي في نفس
الغسالة
أنتظر أن لا يكون في البيت
لا لكي يلمسني بل
لأنه أصبح غريبا
حقاً غريباً.
بعد ان كان
زوجي

Certainly, from that moment on
he would not let me wash my clothes
in the machine that he uses.
I wait until he's out of the house
to use it.
Not because I would like him
to touch me again,
but because he has become a stranger
who was once
my husband.

SONIA

Mère	:	Jacqueline
Père	:	François
Âge	:	29 ans
Profession	:	sans
Domicile	:	Montreuil'

Je commence à avoir peur
de rester dans la maison
quand il y est.

Les souffles de sa respiration me font
    trembler.
À chaque instant il peut se réveiller
pour irriguer la plante de ma peur
avec ses postillons.

Lui, le géant
qui protège les portes de la cave
afin que le rêve ne puisse pas s'enfuir
en souliers de satin
rouge.

سونيا

الأم: جاكلين
الأب: فرنسيس
العمر: 29
المهنة: بدون

بت أخاف أن أمكث
في البيت وهو فيه

أنفاسه تبعث الرعدة في قلبي
في كل لحظة سيستيقظ
ليسقي نبتة خوفي
برذاذ لعابه

هو المارد
الذي يحمي
باب الكهف
لكي لا تقرب منه الأحلام
بأحذية من الساتان
الأحمر

SONIA

Mother	:	Jacqueline
Father	:	François
Age	:	29
Occupation	:	None
Lives in	:	Montreuil

I begin to be afraid
to stay in the house
when he's there.

The puffs of his breath make me tremble.
At any moment he might wake up
to spray the plants of my fear
with his sneezes.

He, the giant who guards the mouth of the cave
so that the dream may not flee
in its shoes
of red satin.

AGNIESKA

Mère	:	Anna
Père	:	Jerzy
Âge	:	38 ans
Profession	:	comédienne

Tout ce qu'il me faut
c'est une chambre
une chambre avec une fenêtre
pour que l'espace puisse y pénétrer
la lune,
    le soleil
        et les étoiles
ainsi que la conversation du monde

Un toit qui me protège des pluies
et des murs pour accrocher les photos
et mon ombre pour ne pas rester seule.

Une chambre, même petite
Je pourrais l'agrandir en faisant sur
    place
mille pas
tournant sur moi en dansant

Une chambre où je pourrais guetter
l'arrivée du temps des cerises
je pourrais rêver de bonheur
et redessiner mes sourires

Une chambre
qui contiendrait
ma liberté.

أغنيسكا

الأم: آننا
الأب: جرزي
العمر: 38
العمل: ممثلة

كل ما أحتاجه
هو غرفة
غرفة بها نافذة يستطيع أن
يدخلها
الشمس
القمر
النجوم
وثرثرات العالم

بسقف يحميني من المطر
وجدران أعلق عليها
صورا
و
ظلي
لكي لا أبقى وحيدة

غرفة ولو صغيرة أ وسعها
بأن أراوح مائة خطوة
وأدور حولي راقصة

غرفة
أستطيع أن أترقب منها
بمجيء فصل الكرز
أستطيع فيها ان أعيد
رسم ابتسامتي و
الحلم بالسعادة.

غرفة تسع
لكل
حريتي

62

AGNIESKA

Mother	:	Anna
Father	:	Jerzy
Age	:	38
Occupation	:	Actress

All that I need
is a room,
a room with a window
through which space can penetrate –
the moon,
    the sun
        and the stars…
the conversation of the world.

A roof to protect against rain
and walls to hang photos on,
and my shadow, so I'm not lonely.

A room, however small.
I can make it bigger,
turning and turning with
a thousand paces,
turning on myself, dancing.

A room where I can await
the arrival of cherry time,
where I can dream of happiness,
redraw my smiles.

A room
that would house
my freedom.

KHADIJA

Âge	:	40 ans
Profession	:	mère au chômage
Diplôme	:	licence de français

خديجة

الأم: زهرة
الأب: عبدالله
العمر: 40
المهنة: أم عاطلة عن الأمومة
الدبلوم: أدب فرنسي

لقد أحببته
الشاب الذي اتى من بلاد الشمس
بلاد أبي وأمي
حاربت الجبال والأنهار
لأجله.
لأجله
توقفت عن الدراسة.
كل ما أقوله غبي
كل ما أطبخه لا يأكل
كثير الملح أو قليله ؟
لأجله
وبسببه
تخليت عن أطفالي
لعلهم يلاقون الطمأنينة
بعيداعن والدين يتشاجران
محاولة رتق التمزق في أحشاء بيتي.

أنا أم في عطالة
ممنوع
أن أمارس أمومتي
أن أحضر لأطفالي الطعام
أن أسمع تنفسهم
وضجيجهم

J'ai aimé
l'homme qui est venu d'un pays de soleil
le pays de mes parents
j'ai fait la guerre
avec les montagnes et les rivières
pour lui.
Pour lui
j'ai arrêté mes études,
tout ce que je disais était idiot.
Tout ce que je cuisinais était trop salé
ou pas assez.
Pour lui
et à cause de lui
j'ai abandonné mes enfants.
Je pensais qu'ils s'épanouiraient mieux
loin des disputes incessantes,
essayant de raccommoder les déchirures
dans les entrailles de la maison.

Mère au chômage,
interdite
d'exercer ma maternité.
Chaque soir je rêve de les étreindre,
je rêve de repriser leurs socquettes,
de préparer leur repas,
d'entendre leur respiration
et leur vacarme.

64

KHADIJA

Age   :   40
Occupation   :   Mother, on the dole
Diploma   :   French teaching licence

I loved
a man from the country of the sun,
my parents' country.
I made war
on the mountains and rivers
for him.
For him,
I quit my studies.
Everything that I said was stupid.
Everything that I'd cook was too salty,
or not salty enough.
Because of him
I abandoned my children,
I thought they might flourish better
away from the incessant arguments,
I was trying to repair the tears
in the entrails of the house.

Unemployed mother,
forbidden
to exercise my motherhood,
every evening I dream of embracing them,
of mending their ankle socks,
preparing their meals,
hearing their breathing,
the noise they make.

J'ai patienté
jusqu'à me trouver
moitié morte sur un lit d'hôpital
cherchant leur visage
et décidée à redevenir
leur mère.

صبرت حتى وجدت نفسي
نصف ميتة في المشفى
أبحث عن وجوههم
مصرة ان اصبح
أمهم

I waited until
I found myself
half dead in a hospital bed,
searching for their faces,
before deciding to become again
their mother.

MADELEINE

Mère	: Ginette
Père	: Maurice
Âge	: 69 ans
Profession	: ancienne mercière

 مادلين

الأم: جينيت
الأب: موريس
العمر: 69
المهنة: بائعة خيطان مفلسة

لم يكن الجو مناسبا
كي تلبس صندلا مكشوفا
أصابع قدميها المعوجة من
الروماتيزم
لايسعها أي حذاء

لم يكن الجو مناسبا
لكي تلبس
مدام ديون
ملابس صيفية
وأن تستلقي كما يستلقي
السواح في يوم قائظ
على الأرصفة

مدام ديون
لديها ولدان
نسيا رقم هاتفها

Le temps n'est pas
à ce qu'elle chausse des sandales
    ouvertes
Ses doigts de pied tordus de rhumatismes
ne peuvent s'enfiler dans aucune
    chaussure

Le temps n'est pas adéquat
pour que madame Dupont
s'habille de vêtements d'été
et s'allonge comme une touriste
les jours de canicule
sur le trottoir.

Madame Dupont a deux enfants.
Ils ont perdu son téléphone.

MADELEINE

Mother   : Ginette
Father   : Maurice
Age   : 69
Occupation : Retired haberdasher

This is not the time
for slipping on open sandals.
Now her toes, tortured with rheumatism,
cannot easily be fitted into any shoes.

It isn't warm enough
for Madame Dupont
to dress in her summer clothes,
to relax like a tourist
in the heatwave
on the pavement.

Madame Dupont has two children.
They have lost her telephone number.

KHAÏRA

Mère   : Bakhta
Père   : Ali
Âge   : 65 ans
Profession   : couturière à la retraite

خيرة

اسم الأم: بختة
الأب: علي
العمر: 65
المهنة: خياطة متقاعدة

زواج أول في ستة عشرة سنة
ثمانية أطفال في سبعة
وعشرين سنة
طلاق أول في الثلاثين
زواج ثان برجل
أعطاها كل الحرية
حتى انه قال لها ذات يوم
فرجك، جسدك لك
افعلي ما تشائين بهما.

فهجرته.

(على الرجل ان يغار على
زوجته
حتى ضربها
قالت
وإلا
فهو لا يحبها.

1er mariage à 16 ans
8 enfants à 27 ans
1er divorce à la trentaine
2ème mariage avec un homme
qui ne lui a jamais demandé
d'où elle venait
ni où elle allait,
un homme qui lui disait:
«Ton sexe est à toi;
Tu peux en faire ce que tu veux».

Alors, elle a demandé le divorce.

«L'homme doit être jaloux de sa femme,»
dit-elle,
«jusqu'à la frapper, au besoin.
Sinon,
c'est qu'il ne l'aime pas.»

KHAÏRA

Mother   :   Bakhta
Father   :   Ali
Age   :   65
Occupation :   Retired seamstress

1st marriage at 16
8 children by age 27
1st divorce at 30.
2nd marriage to a man
who would never ask
where she'd been
nor where she was going,
a man who told her:
'Your sex life is your own business;
you may do as you wish.'

So, she demanded a divorce.

'A man should be jealous of his woman,'
she said,
'even beat her if necessary.
Otherwise
he just doesn't love her.'

TAMARA

Mère	:	Maria
Père	:	Jack
Âge	:	40 ans
Profession	:	peintre

«Tu es zéro
Tu es un sac de sable
Tu es un boulet que je traîne
Tu es incapable de vivre sans moi
Même femme de ménage,
tu ne peux pas faire.

Regarde
tu dis que tu as nettoyé la maison
c'est une poubelle.
Qui va accepter une femme comme
    toi?
Tu ne sais rien faire
même pas l'amour.»

J'ai entendu ça longtemps,
jusqu'à ce que
je le croie.

تمارا

الأم: ماريا
الأب: جاك
العمر: 40
المهنة: رسامة

أنت صِفر
انت كيس من الرمل
انت كرة حديدية أجرجرها
ورائي
كالمساجين
يا لك من مسكينة
حتى عاملة تنظيف لا
تستطعين العمل

انظري
تقولين إنك نظفت البيت
إنه زبالة. .
من سيقبل امرأة مثلك؟
لا تعرفين شيئا
حتى ممارسة الحب
. . . .
سمعت هذا طويلا
حتى
صدّقت. .

72

TAMARA

Mother: :   Maria
Father   :   Jack
Age   :   40
Occupation :   Painter

'You are nothing,
a bag of sand,
a ball and chain
I drag behind me,
you cannot live without me
you don't even know
how to be a housewife.

Look, you say you've cleaned the house –
it's a rubbish tip.
Who could put up with a woman like you,
you don't know how to do anything,
not even how to make love.'

I listened to this
for so long
I began to believe it.

HELENA

Mère	:	Anastasia
Père	:	Vladimir
Âge	:	37 ans
Profession	:	écrivain

Des vêtements qui ne sont pas lavés,
d'autre, propres.
Des feuilles blanches
et d'autres alourdies
de sentiments,
    d'idées,
        de pensées…
Tout, dans un seul bagage que je traîne
d'un lieu à l'autre.

Après que j'ai abandonné ma maison,
mes enfants
et ceux qui étaient ma famille.
J'ai goûté aux autres saveurs de la cruauté,
cruauté du monde
        de la rue
            de la culpabilité
                et des échecs
traînant derrière moi,
    comme un escargot,
        la trace humide de mes regrets.

هيلينا

الأم انستازيا
الأب فلادمير
العمر 37 سنة
المهنة كاتبة

ملابس لم تنظف
وأخرى نظيفة
أوراق بيضاء
وأخرى مثقلة
بمشاعر
وأفكار
أحشرهم في حقيبة واحدة
أجرها من مكان إلى مكان

بعد أن هجرت بيتي
ومن كانوا أهلي
بعد أن هجرت أطفالي

ذقت طعم قسوة أخرى
قسوة العالم
قسوة الطريق
قسوة الوحدة
والذنب

مثل حلزون
اتنقل جارة ورائي
الاثار الرطبة لأسفي

HELENA

Mother   : Anastasia
Father   : Vladimir
Age   : 37
Occupation : Writer

Clothes, some unwashed,
some clean.
Pages, some white and blank,
others weighed down
with feelings,
     ideas,
          thoughts...
All heaped into one bag I drag after me
from one place to another.

After I abandoned my house,
my children
and those who were my family,
I tasted other savours of cruelty,
cruelty of the world,
          of the street,
                    guilt,
                         failures...
tracing along behind me
               like a snail
                    the damp trail of my regrets.

NAÏMA

Mère	:	Fadma
Père	:	Lahcen
Âge	:	30 ans
Profession	:	rien

نعيمة

الأم فاطمة
الأب بنلحسن
العمر 30
المهنة بدون

التلفزيون نعيمة
هو النافذة التي يأتي منها
الهواء
القهوة صباحا
أمام صديقاتها سو إلين
وبروك
بطلات المسلسلات
الحب والمجد والجمال
الذين لا تفهم لغتهن

منذ مجيئها إلى فرنسا
سكنها زوجها في
بيت يغلق بابه عليها بمفتاح
ويمنعها من الخروج
من التحدث الى الجيران
من الابتسام للمرآة
من رؤية التلفزيون
الذي يحرص إخفاء جهاز
التحكم فيه
في مكان صعب المنال

يد نعمة مجروحة
ففي غياب زوجها
تحشرها بألم لتلقط الجهاز
تلعب بأزراره
وتنجح
بأن تهرب من بيتها
عبر تلك الشاشة

La Télé, pour Naïma,
c'est la fenêtre
par où passe l'air,
c'est son café du matin,
avec ses copines Brooke et Sue Helen,
les héroïnes d'*Amour, gloire et beauté*;
pourtant elle ne comprend pas leur langue.

Depuis qu'elle est arrivée en France
Naïma vit dans une maison
qui se ferme à clef
chaque fois que son mari en sort.

Naïma n'a pas le droit d e sortir,
de parler aux voisins,
de sourire devant le miroir
ni de regarder la télé
(dont il a caché la télécommande
dans un coin inaccessible).

Naïma se blesse la main
en l'absence de son mari
en la glissant dans la fente du meuble
pour la récupérer
Elle tripote ses boutons
et réussit
à s'évader de sa maison
à travers l'écran.

NAÏMA

Mother   : Fadma
Father   : Lahcen
Age   : 30
Occupation : None

The TV, for Naïma,
is a window
the air passes through.
It is her morning coffee
with her pals Brook and Sue Helen,
the heroines of *Love, Glory and Beauty*,
never mind that she doesn't speak
their language.

Since she arrived in France,
Naïma has lived in a house
she locks with a key
every time her husband goes out.

Naïma is not allowed to go out,
to talk to the neighbours,
to smile before the mirror
or to watch TV
(so he has stashed the control
in an inaccessible place).

Naïma injured her hand
in her husband's absence,
slipping it through a gap in the furniture
to retrieve the remote.
Fiddling with the buttons,
she escapes
from the house
          through the screen.

MONICA ET LES AUTRES

Sur les trottoirs du monde,
sous son soleil écrasant
ou sous les néons d'une chambre,
Monica, Nawal, Maya, Aïcha, Laura,
    Sandra et Yoko
dans le froid
et ses caresses rêches,
habillées du vêtement léger de leur peau,
ont transformé leurs corps
en boutiques
dans lesquelles
elles marchandent.

Vendeuses de plaisir
pour ceux qui sont en manque,
elles touchent
ceux que personne ne touche
et donnent un instant de tendresse
(peut-être)
à ceux qui n'y ont jamais droit.

Argent...
                    argent...
                                    argent...
en échange
de vingt ou trente minutes
pendant lesquelles
Monica, Nawal, Maya, Aïcha, Laura,
    Sandra et Yoko

ouvrent leurs boutiques
et ferment les yeux.

مونيكا والأخريات

على أرصفة العالم
تحت شمسه الحارقة
أوتحت ضوء النيون الأزرق
لغرفة
تقف
مونيكا نوال مايا خديجة لورا
وساندرا
يوكو

بملابس خفيفة
هي جلدهن
أمام البرد وملساته الخشنة
أجسادهن تحولت
لدكاكين
يتاجرن فيها
لمن يرغب الشراء

بائعات اللذة
لمن يحتاج
تلمسن محرومي الحب
تمنحن لحظات من الحنان
لمن ليس لهم الحق

مال. .
    مال. .
        مال
مقابل
عشرين أو ثلاثين دقيقة
تفتح
مونيكا و نوال ماياو ايشا و
لورا ساندرا
يوكو
دكانهن
وتغمضن عيونهن

On the pavements of the world,
under its crushing sun
or under neon lights in a room,
Monica, Nawal, Maya, Aïcha, Laura, Sandra and Yoko,
in the cold,
in its rough caress,
dressed in the light garments of their skin,
have turned their bodies
into shops
in which they haggle.

Vendors of pleasure
to those who lack it,
they touch
those whom nobody touches
and give a moment's tenderness
(perhaps)
to those who had never earned it.

Money…

        money…

                money…

in exchange for
twenty or thirty minutes
during which
Monica, Nawal, Maya, Aïcha, Laura, Sandra and Yoko

open their shops
and close their eyes.

VOILE

Tu passes,
comme si le noir d'un corbeau t'habillait
t'enlaçant dans ses ailes.
Tu as jeté un voile épais
sur ton corps,
    corps du désir,
        corps du péché.
           maison de Satan.

Soumise,
tu retournes dans le ventre du néant,
acceptant d'être gommé.
Tu n'es plus là.

tchador   linceul
        enveloppe
prison   tombe

Loin des yeux du soleil,
    du vent et de la brise,
        loin des yeux de la vie,
tu passes
voleur effrayé
tu voles
le peu d'air
qu'ils te laissent respirer

Tu marches
Autour de toi: mille murs
et murs
mille obscurités
et nuit

الحجاب

تمرين . .
غراب أسود
يلبسك
يضمك بجناحيه
يلف جسدك
جسد الشهوة
جسد الخطيئة
بيت الشيطان
فصدقت
تعودين لبطن العدم
راضية أن تُمحَيْ
حجاب .   عباءة
تشادور
غطاء .   قبر

محجوبة عن
عيون الشمس
عن الريح والنسائم
عن عيون الحياة

تمرين
لصاً جباناً
تسرقين الهواءالقليل
الذي رضوا ان تستنشقيه

تمشين
وحولك ألف جدار
وجدار
وألف عتمة
و عتمةٍ

VEIL

You pass by,
as if robed in the black of a crow,
wrapped in its wings.
You have thrown a heavy veil
over your body,
          body of desire,
                    body of sin,
                              house of Satan.

Submissive,
you return to the womb of being,
you accept being erased,
you are no longer there.

chador   shroud
                    envelope
prison   tomb

Far from the eyes of the sun,
the wind, and the breeze,
far from the eyes of life
you pass by,
a frightened thief,
you steal what little air
they let you breathe.

You walk past.
Around you there are thousands
and thousands of walls,
a thousand darknesses,
night.

Ô bel être
mère de la vie
et sa fille

refuse le néant.

أيها الكائن الجميل
أم الحياة
وابنتها

ارفضي العدم.

O beautiful being,
mother and daughter
of life,

refuse this nothingness, refuse!

GAZA

Mère : Palestine
Père : le monde
Âgée comme la Terre
Profession : survivre

غزة

الأم: فلسطين
الاب: العالم
العمر: قِدم الأرض
المهنة: البقاء

Là-bas
chaque jour un homme,
Et une femme qui voit en lui,
comme toutes les femmes de la Terre,
un être cher et beau,
un homme ensanglanté
qui gît sur une civière
au lieu de grandir et de vivre
comme tous les enfants de la Terre.

هناك
في كل يوم يسقط رجل
لأمرأة ترى طفلها
ككل امهات
غاليا وجميلا
مضرجا بالدم
محمولا على خشبة الموت
بدل ان يكبر ويهرم
ككل اطفال الأرض .

Gaza crie:
«Mon ventre, porteur de vie,
déchiqueté
comme le corps de mes parents,
le corps de mes frères
            et de mes enfants.

غزة تصرخ
بطني حامل الحياة
ممزقا
كأجساد أبائي
و أخوتي
وابنائي.

À la place des cadeaux,
sous le sapin,
leurs corps
empaquetés dans le papier cadeau de
     la mort.

بدل الهدايا تحت اشجار
الصنوبر
في الأعياد
أجسادهم ملفوفة بورق هديا
الموت

À la place des guirlandes qui illuminent
les rues du monde,
mes rues sont éclairées
par les bombes.

بدل الأنوار المضيئة في شوارع
العالم
شوارعي تضيئها
القنابل

GAZA

Mother   : Palestine
Father   : The world
As old as the Earth
Occupation : Survival

Over there
every day there is a man,
and a woman who sees in him,
as do all the women of Earth,
a being both dear and beautiful.
A man covered in blood
who lies on a stretcher
instead of growing and living
like all the children of Earth.

Gaza cries out:
'My womb, carrier of life,
torn
as the bodies of my parents,
the bodies of my brothers
       and of all my children.

Instead of gifts
under the fir tree
their bodies wrapped
in the gaudy
paper of death.

In place of the tinsel brightening
the streets of the world
my streets are lit up
by bombs.

بدل الماء في الصنابر
تجري دماء شبابي واطفالي
حتى الفئران في منزلي جائعة
وعطشى

دمار
دما ر

صراخ
وصراخ

لا يصل
لآذان السموات
في إجازة بمناسبة الأعياد

ولا لعيون الأنبياء
المنشغلين برؤية
مباراة كرة

وأنا
احتضر
احتضر

و لا من يبالي . .

À la place de l'eau,
des robinets,
coule le sang de mes adolescents.

Même les rats, dans ma maison,
ont faim et soif.

Destruction,
        destruction,

hurlements,
        hurlements,

Mais ils ne parviennent pas
aux oreilles du Ciel,
en congé pour les Fêtes.

Ni aux yeux des prophètes,
en train de regarder
un match de foot.

Et moi,
j'agonise,
        j'agonise

et personne ne s'en soucie.»

Instead of water,
from the taps there flows
the blood of my teenagers.

Even the rats, in my house,
are hungry and thirsty.

Destruction,
          destruction,

Howling,
          howling,

But this does not reach
the ears of heaven –
everyone's on vacation –

nor does it reach the eyes of the prophets –
caught up in watching
a game of football –

And me,
I am dying,
          I am dying

and nobody notices.'

II
THE SCREAM

FLORA

Fille de Florence
Âge : 6 ans

Je n'aime pas
aller à l'école

J'ai peur de rentrer
et de ne plus trouver
ma maman.

فلورا

ابنة فلورانس
العمر: 6

لا أحب الذهاب
إلى المدرسة.

أخاف أن اعود
ولا أجد
أمي.

FLORA

Daughter of Florence
Age : 6

I do not like
going to school.

I'm afraid I'll come home
and never again
find my mother.

سيف

ابن زهرة
العمر 10 سنوات

رأيت أمي تبكي
وهي تحضر العشاء

ماذا يبكيك يا أمي
تقولين البصل
ولا يوجد بصل
بين يديك.

Fils de Zohra
Âge : 10 ans

J'ai vu ma mère pleurer
tandis qu'elle préparait
le dîner.

Qui te fait pleurer maman?
Tu dis que c'est l'oignon
et il n'y a pas d'oignon
dans tes mains…

SEF

Son of Zohra
Age : 10

I saw my mother weeping
while she was preparing
dinner.

What has made you cry, Mother?
You say it's the onion
and there is no onion
in your hands...

SARA

Fille de Sana
Âge : 9 ans

سارة

ابنة سناء
العمر 9

Pourquoi mon père
bat ma mère?

Elle ne sait pas bien repasser
ses chemises.

Moi, quand je serais grande
je repasserai les chemises
très bien.

– لماذا يضرب أبي
أمي؟
لأنها لا تعرف أن تكوي
قمصانه

أنا، عندما سأصبح كبيرة
سأكوي القمصان
جيدا

SARA

Daughter of Sana
Age : 9

Why does my father
beat my mother?

She does not know
how to iron his shirts properly.

Me, when I'm grown up
I will iron the shirts
very well.

BARTOSH

Fils de Agnieska
Âge : 10 ans

Maman
dans la nuit mon lit entend
des cris
Il se mouille
il pense que vous vous disputez.

Eh! maman
dis que tu as dormi
et oublié
d'éteindre
la télé.

بارتروك

ابن اغنيسكا
العمر 10

ماما
في الليل يسمع سريري
صراخاً
فيتبلل.
يظن انكما تتشاجران؟

هه ماما
قولي لي
بأنك نمت ناسية
أن تطفئي
التلفزيون؟

BARTOSH

Son of Agnieska
Age : 10

Mother,
at night my bed hears
crying,
it wets itself,
it thinks you are arguing.

Eh! Mother,
tell me you fell asleep
and forgot
to turn off
the TV.

FAÂDI

Fils de Sonia
Âge : 7 ans

Tu sais maman
si pendant la nuit
le géant vient
pour te frapper
tu peux venir
dormir dans mon lit.

J'ai bien mangé ma soupe
et tous les épinards
pour que vite
je devienne grand
et que je te protège

فادي

ابن سونيا
العمر 7 سنوات

أتعرفين يا أمي
تستطيعين أن تنامي
في سريري
إذا جاء الوحش
ليضربك

لقد شربت كل الحساء
وأكلت كل السبانخ
لكي —بسرعة— أصبح كبيرا
وأحميك.

FAÂDI

Son of Sonia
Age : 7

You know, Mother,
if the giant comes
during the night
to beat you,
you can come
sleep in my bed.

I ate up all my soup
and all my spinach
so that
I can grow up quickly
and protect you.

SALMA

Fille de Leila
Âge : 9 ans

Pourquoi tu ne vas pas chez le médecin
pour qu'il te rende ton sourire,
ton joli sourire,
maman?

سلمى

ابنة ليلى
العمر9

لماذا لا تذهبين إلى الطبيب
ليعيد لك ابتسامتك
ابتسامتك العذبة
يا أمي.

SALMA

Daughter of Leila
Age : 9

Why don't you go to the doctor
and have him give you back your smile,
Mother,
your lovely smile?

SAMIR

Fils de Magda
Âge : 13 ans

سمير

الأم: ماجدة
العمر 13

Je ne me souviens pas de son visage,
J'étais petit quand mon père
m'a emmené chez ma grand-mère
loin
très loin.

لا أذكر وجهها
كنت صغيرا عندما
أخذني أبي لجدتي
بعيدا جداً جداً

Ma grand-mère n'aime pas
celle qui m'a mis au monde,
À chaque prière, elle demande à Dieu
de la punir.

جدتي لا تحب
التي أنجبتني
في كل صلاة تطلب الله
أن يعاقبها

Elle disait que son sang est celui du
        diable.
Et qu'elle m'a abondonné
pour que les chats me mangent.

اسمعها تقول بأن دم أمي من
دم شيطان
وبأنها تخلت عني
لتأكلني القطط ؟

Dix-huit mois… c'est très jeune
pour qu'un enfant
puisse se défendre.

ثمانية عشر شهرا، عمر صغير
لكي يستطيع طفل
أن يدافع عن نفسه. .

SAMIR

Son of Magda
Age : 13

I do not remember her face,
I was very small when my father
carried me off to my Grandmother's house
far,
far away.

My Grandmother did not like
the one who had brought me into the world,
with every prayer she would demand that God
would punish her.

She would say, hers is the blood of the devil.
She would say, she abandoned you
for the cats to eat you up.

Eighteen months old... that's very young
for a child
to have to defend himself.

CLÉMENT ET ROMAIN

Enfants de Florence
Âge : 12 et 9 ans

N'oublie pas, maman,
de me mettre avec mon frère
dans ton bagage.

On va pas t'embêter
on sera sage, cette fois.

كليمان و رومان

الأم فلورنس
العمر 12 و 9

لا تنسي يا أمي
أن تضعيني وأخي
في حقيبتك.

نقسم بإننا لن نعذبك
سنكون عقلاء جداً هذه
المرة.

CLÉMENT AND ROMAIN

Children of Florence
Age : 12 and 9

Don't forget, Mother,
to pack me and my brother
in your baggage.

We won't annoy you,
we'll behave this time.

CHLOË

Fille de Suzanne
Âge : 11 ans

كلوة

ابنة سوزان
العمر 11

كنت أرى أبي
شادا شعر أمي
جارا إياها الى
الحمام
فأختبئ في الخزانة
حتى ينتهي العراك

في وسط الصالون
صورة تمساح
سميناه وأخوتي
بابا

J'ai souvent
vu mon père
tirer maman par les cheveux
jusqu'à la salle de bain
alors je me cachais
dans le placard
en attendant que ça se calme.

Sur le mur du salon:
la photo d'un crocodile.
Avec mes frères
on l'appelle
«Papa».

CHLOË

Daughter of Suzanne
Age : 11

I have often
seen my father
drag my mother by the hair
into the bathroom.
I'd hide myself
in the cupboard
and wait until he'd calm down.

On the wall in the sitting room
there's the photo of a crocodile.
Myself and my brother,
we used to call it
'Papa'.

III
WITH EVERY BEGINNING

L'AMOUR

I

L'amour aurait dû
s'agripper à une planche
pour flotter
ou construire une arche
pour sauver ses sujets
Mais,
comme un voyageur toujours en partance,
comme les chassures d'un coureur
il préfère s'en aller
laissant derrière lui
    fleuves,
        montagnes,
            chanson et imprécations,
pour chercher
de nouveaux commencements
et des fins tristes.

الحب

1

كان على الحب
أن يتمسك بخشبة
أو أن يبني سفينة
لينقذ رعاياه
ولكنه
كرحالة متأهب دائما للسفر
كبوط عداء
يفضل الرحيل
تاركا وراءه
الأنهار
والجبال
الأغانيوالأشعار
للبحث عن بدايات جديدة

LOVE

I

Love
should have grabbed a board
to float,
or built an ark
to save its subjects,
but like a traveller always outward bound,
like the shoes of a runner,
it prefers to head on out
leaving behind it
      rivers,
            mountains,
                  songs and entreaties,
to search out
new beginnings
and sad endings.

2

لم نعد نبكي من أجله
نتركه يذهب
بدون أن نصطحبه الى الباب
كضيف عزيز

نراقبه من خلف النافذة
وهو يجرجر حقائبه
ملقيا علينا نظرة من يرغب
أن نهرع
لنسقط تحت قدميه
متوسلينه أن يبقى

نتركه يذهب
بدون ضجة
بضعة آهات مكبوتة
بضعة عضات على شفاهنا
وبضعة دمعات مكبوحة
لنليق به نحن الضحايا
وكأننا أصبحنا
مدمنين

II

On ne pleure plus pour lui
On le laisse partir
sans l'accompagner à la porte
comme on le ferait d'un hôte cher

Nous observons
derrière les rideaux
pendant qui'il traîne lentement ses bagages
et qu'il nous jette un regard
désirant qu'on courre
pour tomber à ses pieds
le suppliant de rester

On le laisse partir
sans bruit
Quelque soupir étouffé
    quelque morsure sur nos lèvres
      et quelques larmes
pour mériter d'être ses victimes
comme si
nous nous étions accoûtumés
à son abandon.

II

We weep no more for him,
we let him leave
without accompanying him to the door
as one would a cherished guest.

We watch from behind the curtains
as he drags his suitcase slowly behind him
until he glances back at us,
hoping we'll run after him,
fall at his feet,
beg him to stay.

We let him go
without a sound – perhaps
a few stifled sighs
    a bitten lip
        a few tears
to earn being his victims,
as if we were accustomed
to his abandoning us.

Chaque fois, on l'offre
oubliant ses anciennes douleurs
croyant qu'il va être sauvé cette fois-ci

On dissimule ses blessures avec de la
    couleur
on les décore avec des fleurs
on le présente comme s'il était neuf
et commençait à battre
à l'instant

On jure
y croyant nous-mêmes
que nous n'avons jamais connu
de tels sentiments auparavant
tellement heureux de trouver
celui qui va
l'accepter
celui qui va
le chérir
et peut-être
ce qui va
le blesser
à nouveau.

3

في كل مرة نمنحه
ناسين آلامه الماضية
معتقدين أننا
سننجو به هذه المرة

نمّوه جروحه بالألوان
نرسم عليها زهورا
ونقدمه وكأنه جديد
قد بدأ ينبض
للتو

مقسمين
ومصدقين أنفسنا
أننا لم نعرف أحاسيس كهذه
من قبل
فرحين أننا قد وجدنا
من
سيتلقفه
من سيحضنه
ومن ربما
سيجرحه
من جديد

III

Over and over we make the offer,
forgetting old pain,
believing that this time he can be saved.

We hide his wounds with colours,
decorate them with flowers,
we present him
as if he were nine
and was beginning
to beat at time.

We swear,
and we believe ourselves,
that we have never known
such feelings before,
so happy to have found
one who will accept,
one who will cherish
and perhaps one
who will wound
again.

IV

Parce qu'il ne sent pas toujours
l'eau de rose
que souvent
il n'est pas
si léger
qu'il est parfois
fatigué
et qu'il dort
la bouche ouverte

Parce ce que sa tête se couvre de
        cendres
ses oreilles s'habillent de coton
que la veilleuse de ses yeux s'affablit
et se perd l'albatros de son regard

Parce que l'amour vieillit
et comme nous
il meurt.

4

لأنه لا يفوح دائما
برائحة المسك
لأنه غالبا
لا يكون خفيفا
لأنه أحيانا
يكون متعبا
لأنه ينام فاتحا فمه
لأن شعره يتغطى بالرماد
لأن سمعه يلبس القطن
لأن منارة عينيه تخبو
و نوارسه تضيع

لأن الحب يشيخ
ومثلنا
يموت

IV

Because he does not always smell
the rose water,
because often he is not
so light,
because he is sometimes
tired
and sleeps
with his mouth open

Because his head is covered with ashes,
because his ears are covered with cotton,
the pilot of his vision weakens,
and he loses the albatross gaze of his eyes

Because love ages him
and like us
he must die

V

La peau qui se ramollit
l'amour la voit

Les fesses alourdies
l'amour les voit

Les seins qui se vident
le ventre mou
et les rides de la vieillesse
l'amour les voit

Il voit
les dents noircies,
    les cicatrices,
        les vergetures
            le teint terni
mais
il ferme les yeux sur tout cela
satisfait
de sa propre beauté.

5

الجلد الذي يتهدل
الحب يرى

الأرداف الثقيلة
الحب يرى

الصدر الهابط
الحب يرى
البطن الممزق
وتجاعيد الشيخوخة
الحب يرى

يرى
الأسنان المسودة
يرى الجروح
والتشقق

إلا أنه
يغمض عينيه عن كل هذا
مكتفيا
بجماله.

v

The skin grown soft,
love sees it.
The buttocks sagging,
love sees it.

The empty breasts,
the slack belly
and the wrinkles of age,
love sees it.

Love sees
the blackened teeth
     the scars
          the stretch marks
               the blemished complexion

but
closes its eyes
satisfied
with its own beauty.

Regarde, regarde
toutes ces blessures que j'ai reçues
au cours de tes combats.

Cette blessure, profonde et foncée,
je'ai eu à 18 ans;
la première fois que tu m'as blessée.
J'ai saigné jusqu'à penser mourir,
jurant ne plus jamais
m'engager dans un autre combat.

Mais chaque fois tu reviens,
souriant de ce sourire-là,
promettant paradis et éternité

Alors j'y retourne,
sans heaume et sans armure…
Quand, soudain, tu tires la langue
me poignardant autant que tu peux:
comme si tu voulais vraiment
ma mort.

Je ne sais par quel miracle
j'en réchappe,
ni par quel miracle
je retombe dans ton arène.

Regarde, regarde
celle-ci est encore fraîche,
elle saigne encore,
Sois tendre, cette fois-ci…

6

انظر انظر
الى كل الجروح
لتي أصبت بها في معاركك

هذا الجرح العميق الغامق
كان عمري 18 عشرة عاما
عندما جرحتني
نزفت حتى ظننت أنني
سأموت
قاسمة أنني لن أخوض معركة
أخرى

في كل مرة تأتيني
مبتسما ابتسامتك تلك
واعدا بالجنة والأبد

فأعود بدون خوذة ولا درع
واذا بك تمد لي لسانك
طاعنا ما استطعت
وكأنك تريد حقا
أجلي
لا أدري بأي أعجوبة
أنجو
ولا بأي أعجوبة
أقع في حلبتك؟

انظر انظر
إلى هذا الاخير انه ما زال
طريا
ما زال ينزف. .

رُفقا بي هذه المرة

Look, look
at all the wounds I have received
in your wars.

This wound, deep and dark,
I got it at 18,
the first time you injured me.
I bled until I thought I might die,
swore I would never again
get into a fight.

But every time you return,
smiling that smile,
promising paradise and eternity,

back I come again
without helmet or armour
and you lunge at me with your words,
stabbing as hard as you can,
as if, truly,
you wished me dead.

I do not know by what miracle
I survive,
nor by what miracle
I fall back into your arena.

Look, look,
this one is still fresh,
still bleeding.
Be gentle, this time…

Tu vois:
il n'y a plus de place pour une autre
    blessure.
Ou alors,
fais-le joliment.

فكما ترى لم يعد هناك
مكان لجرح آخر
وإن لم فاجعله
جميلاً

You see,
I cannot bear another wound.
At the very least, do it nicely.

VII

De lui, on attend
tout
Et sur ses épaules, on pose tous les poids
Est-ce qu'il guérit des maladies?
Est-ce qu'il répare les os cassés?
Est-ce qu'il traite les rhumatismes?

De lui, on attend
tout:
changer la couleur de la mer
arrêter les tempêtes
éteindre le feu…

Mais
est-ce que l'amour gérit de l'amour?

Ah! Comme si
il était capable de miracle.

7

منه ننتظر
كل شيء
وعلى عاتقه نضعكل الأحمال
ولكن
هل يشفي من وجع الرأس ؟
هل يرمم العظم؟
هل يداوي القهر؟

منه ننتظر كل شيء
تغيير لون البحر والمحيط
التحليق بدون اجنحة
إيقاف العواصف ،المطر
والنيران؟

لكن؟
هل يشفي الحب من الحب؟

أه وكأنه قادر حقا على
المعجزات

From him, we expect
everything.
On his shoulders, we can place any weight.
Can he heal diseases?
Can he repair broken bones?
Can he treat rheumatism?

From him we expect
everything:
change the colour of the sea
halt storms in their tracks
extinguish fires…

But,
can love heal love?

Ah, if so
it would be capable of miracles.

La fin
je la connais par avance,
je la vois arriver
de manière inéluctable,
déguisée sous des visages
devenus familiers,
répétant des mots
que je commence à savoir par cœur.

Elle vient lentement
ou hâtivement
jusqu'à en oublier
de mettre ses chaussures.

La fin
a le toucher
du poil d'un chat
que j'ai élevé dans mes bras…
Je ruse, la calme, la dorlote, la supplie,
pour la faire patienter…
Mais elle,
elle ne m'attend pas.

La fin
dans son amertume,
a un goût mystérieux
de commencement.

8

أعرفها مقدماً
أراها آتية لا محالة
متنكرة بوجوه ألفتها
متزينة ما أمكنها
مرددة كلمات حفظتها على
ظهر قلب

بطيئة تأتي
أم سريعة
تنسى حتى
أن تنتعل حذاءها.

النهايات لها رائحة ألفتها
كرائحة إبطي
وملمس قطةٍ
ربيتها في حضني.
أهدئها
ألاطفها
أتوسل إليها
أتحايل عليها
أبكي
أمهلها ولا تمهلني.

النهايات
في مرارتها طعمٌ غامض
لبدايات قادمة . .

VIII

The end –
I know it before it comes,
I watch it arrive
in its inevitable manner
disguised under faces
become familiar,
repeating words
I have begun to know by heart.

It comes slowly,
or hastily as if
it had forgotten
to put on its shoes.

The end –
it's like stroking the fur
of a cat held in my arms.
I trick, I calm, I pamper, I beseech
to quieten it
but love,
love is not listening.

The end
in its bitterness
has the mysterious taste
of some beginning.

CE SONT ELLES...

Ce sont elles
qui t'ont porté
qui t'ont offert leur sang et leur utérus
qui t'ont mis au monde
qui t'ont lavé
qui t'ont allaité

Ce sont elles
qui t'ont chéri
quand tu étais petit
jusqu'à ce que tu deviennes grand
quand tu étais faible
jusqu'à ce que tu deviennes fort

Ce sont elles
qui t'ont désiré
qui t'ont enlacé
qui t'ont accueilli dans leur ventre
t'ont donné leur bouche
t'ont fait boire de leur eau

Ce sont elles
qui t'ont trahi
et qui t'ont
abandonné.

هن

هن اللواتي حملن بك
قاسمنك دماءهن
و ارحامهن

هن
اللواتي أنجتك
اللواتي غسلنك
اللواتي أرضعنك

هن
اللواتي رعينك
وأنت صغيرا
حتى صرت كبيرا
ضعيفا حتى صرت قويا هن
اللواتي رغبنك
ووهبنك أفواههن
و مائهن
اللواتي شاركنك أجسادهن
اللواتي استقبلنك في بطونهن

هن
اللواتي أحببنك
اللواتي
حنك
و
هجرنك

THERE ARE WOMEN...

There are women
who carried you
who offered their blood and their wombs
who brought you into the world
who bathed you
who breastfed you

There are women
who cherished you
when you were small
until you grew up,
when you were weak
until you became strong

There are women
who desired you
who entwined you in their arms
who welcomed you in their wombs
who gave you their mouths
who gave you to drink of their water

There are women
who betrayed you
and there are women who
abandoned you.

أريد أن أكون

Je voudrais être une femme.
Signe distinctif:
un sourire éternel sur les lèvres
des baisers
profond comme le miel.

امرأة
علامتها الفارقة
ابتسامة أبدية على فمها
قبلات
عذبة تقطر من شفاهها

Je voudrais être une femme
qu'on ne peut ni additionner
ni soustraire
ni multiplier
ni diviser
ni gommer
ni sommer
ni assommer.

أريد أن أكون
امرأة
لا تجمع
لا تطرح
لا تضرب
لا تجزأ
لا تكسر
لا تمحى

I WOULD LIKE TO BE A WOMAN

I would like to be a woman.
Distinguishing marks:
an eternal smile on the lips,
kisses
deep as honey.

I would like to be a woman
to whom
nothing is added,
from whom
nothing is subtracted
not multiplied
not divided
not erased
not overcome.

MERCI À TOUS CEUX...

Merci à tous ceux
qui m'ont aimée
et tous ceux qui m'ont détestée
ceux qui m'ont abandonnée
et ceux que j'ai abandonnés

Chaque fois ils m'ont redonné du feu
et attisé en moi le désir

Il y a ceux que j'ai oubliés
et ceux que je n'oublierai jamais

Ils ne m'ont pas empêchée
de m'aventurer
chaque fois
à aimer de nouveau.

أشكرهم جميعهم

من أحبني
ومن كرهني
منهجرني
ومن هجرت

في كل مرة
أعادوا لي النار
وبعثوا في جسدي الحياة

هناك من نسيتهم
وهناك من لم أنسهم

إلا أنهم
لم ولن يمنعوني
أن أغامر
وفي كل مرة
أن أحب من جديد

I THANK THEM ALL

Thank you to all those
who have loved me
and all those who have hated me,
those who abandoned me
and all those I abandoned.

All of you restored the fire in me,
all of you fuelled desire in me.

There are those I have forgotten,
and those whom I will never forget.

None of you ever prevented me
from venturing,
time after time,
once more into love.

Maram al-Masri is from Lattakia in Syria, now settled in Paris. She studied English Literature at Damascus University before starting publishing her poetry in Arab magazines in the 1970s. Today she is considered one of the most acknowledged, influential and captivating feminine voices of her generation and to date her work has been translated into eleven languages, including French, German, English, Italian , Spanish, Serbian, Corsican and Turkish.

In addition to numerous poems published in literary journals, several Arab anthologies and various international anthologies, she has published four collections of poems, the first of which, *I Threaten You with a White Dove*, appeared in 1987. Her second collection, *A Red Cherry on a White-tiled Floor*, followed ten years later in 1997 and was published in French translation by Éditions PHA in 2003. It was also translated into English by Khaled Mattawa and published in a bilingual edition in 2004 by Bloodaxe Books. In 2007, the publishing house Al Manar released her third collection, *I Look at You*, a book that was initially published in Beirut and which was awarded the Prix de la Poésie de la SGDL. Her fourth collection, *Barefoot Souls*, published in 2009, won the Prix des Découvreurs in 2011, and the Prix Poés Yvelines in the same year.

Maram al-Masri has participated in many international festivals of poetry in France and abroad, including the first-ever Arab author event at the Dublin Writers Festival, 2004. She is the recipient of a number of prestigious literary prizes, including the Adonis Prize of the Lebanese Cultural Forum for the best creative work in Arabic in 1998, the Premio Citta di Calopezzati for the section Poesie de la Mediterranée, the Prix d'Automne 2007 of the Société des gens de letters, Il Fiore d'Argento 2015 for cultural excellence and the Premio Laurentum per la Poesia 2015, Dante Alighieri award.

THEO DORGAN was born in Cork in 1953. He is a poet who is also a novelist, non-fiction prose writer, editor, translator, broadcaster, librettist and documentary scriptwriter. He has published five books of poetry. His most recent collections are *Greek*, published in 2012 and *Nine Bright Shiners*, published in 2014, both from Dedalus Press.

His two prose accounts of crossing the Atlantic under sail, *Sailing for Home* (Penguin Ireland) and *Time on the Ocean; A Voyage from Cape Horn to Cape Town* (New Island Books), won wide acclaim, as has his recently published first novel, *Making Way* (New Island Books, 2013).

His translations of the Slovenian poet Barbara Korun, *Songs of Earth and Light*, were published by Southword Editions in 2005.

His own work has been translated into many languages. Two full collections have been published in Italian, and a selected poems in French. *La hija de Safo* was published by Ediciones Hiperion, Madrid, in 2001

He has been editor of, among other titles, *Irish Poetry since Kavanagh, A Book of Uncommon Prayer*, the anthologies *La paume ouverte, What We Found There* and *Watching the River Flow* and, with Gene Lambert, *Leabhar Mór na hÉireann / The Great Book of Ireland*, a unique manuscript volume on vellum.

He is a member of Aosdána.

ARC PUBLICATIONS
publishes translated poetry in bilingual editions
in the following series:

ARC TRANSLATIONS
Series Editor Jean Boase-Beier

'VISIBLE POETS'
Series Editor Jean Boase-Beier

ARC CLASSICS:
NEW TRANSLATIONS OF GREAT POETS OF THE PAST
Series Editor Jean Boase-Beier

ARC ANTHOLOGIES IN TRANSLATION
Series Editor Jean Boase-Beier

'NEW VOICES FROM EUROPE & BEYOND'
(anthologies)
Series Editor Alexandra Büchler

details of which can be found on the
Arc Publications website at
www.arcpublications.co.uk